THE WAGES OF OBSESSIVE MATERIALISM

Ayo Banjo, FNAL

Edited by

B. Olatunji Oloruntimehin

Occasional Publication of

THE NIGERIAN ACADEMY OF LETTERS

Number 5

Ayo Banjo FNAL

THE WAGES OF OBSESSIVE
MATERIALISM

Published by

The Nigerian Academy of Letters

Faculty of Arts, University of Ibadan

Ibadan, Nigeria

Copyright © 2008 Nigerian Academy of Letters

Published in August 2008

ISBN-13: 978-1535336208

ISBN-10: 153533620X

Editor's Note

THE WAGES OF OBSESSIVE MATERIALISM
here presented, is the text of the NAL Convocation
Lecture which Professor Ayo Banjo delivered in 2007.

Professor Ayo Banjo, FNAL, is Emeritus Professor of
English, University of Ibadan, Ibadan.

A former Vice-Chancellor of the University of Ibadan,
Professor Banjo is also a Past President of the Nigerian
Academy of Letters (NAL).

Editor

THE WAGES OF OBSESSIVE MATERIALISM

By

Ayo Banjo, FNAL

'The greatest happiness of the greatest number' is the Utilitarian philosophy associated with the name of the English philosopher Jeremy Bentham (1806-1873). By this philosophy, an action is considered good if it increases pleasure, and bad if it increases pain. Contemporary politicians explicitly or implicitly, or perhaps just supposedly, make this the guiding principle of governance, but its weakness was highlighted by another British philosopher, Thomas Carlyle (1875-1881) who described Bentham's proposal as 'pig philosophy' because, according to him, 'it appeared to base the goal of ethics on the swinish pleasures of the multitude.'

John Stuart Mill, for his own part, in attempting to refine Bentham's philosophy, postulated a distinction between higher pleasures and lower pleasures. He put it graphically by saying 'Better to be Socrates dissatisfied than a fool satisfied.' For him, the lower pleasures were pleasures of the flesh, whereas the higher pleasures were pleasures of the intellect.

Immanuel Kant's Categorical Imperative, however, offers us a more acceptable alternative. Kant 'universalises' morality. According to Roger Jones:

> 'What Kant means .... is that, the way that we judge an action to be moral is to universalise it: if I want to know if telling a !e on a particular occasion is justifiable, 1 must try to imagine what would happen if everyone was to lie. Kant thinks that any rational being

would agree that a world in which there is no lying is preferable to one in which lying was common; in a society in which lying was common no one could trust the word of anyone else.'

Thus it would be necessary to combine Kant's Categorical Imperative with John Stuart Mill's refinement of Bentham's Utilitarianism to arrive at a moral guide in the governance of any country. The extent to which governments, particularly in developing countries, are strongly moved by ethical considerations is in doubt, but Bentham's Utilitarianism is obviously a vote-catcher, if even as an unfulfilled promise.

It is correctly assumed that the chief function of a government is to enable every citizen to improve his lot in life. To this end, the government is supposed to care for the material as well as spiritual well-being of the citizens. But since material well-being is obviously more easily measurable than spiritual well-being, most governments feel that they should be concerned with only material well-being, leaving spiritual matters, in any case, in the hands of religious organizations. We all know what Nigerians mean when they talk about 'the dividends of democracy.' They are obviously not clamouring for more Churches and Mosques to be opened. Indeed, new Churches are opened every day in the country, with results that are truly baffling. As for governments, it is fashionable for them to descry be their States as secular States, emphasizing the separation of politics or governance, and religion. Recent events in Turkey remind us of the passion that the prospects of the mixture of politics with religion can generate.

The laws of a country are, hopefully, based on ethical foundations. No country that we know of rewards individuals for committing murder or robbing their fellow citizens; but the State does not consider it its business to inquire into the morality of the citizen's action provided the laws of the land have been at least technically observed. All too often in the developing world, the State is more concerned for its citizens to be happy than for them to be good. And it concentrates, not on the pleasures of the intellect, but on those of the flesh.

If the government considers individuals' morality to be none of its business, it is legitimate to ask what the agency, to which that responsibility has been remitted, is doing about it. There are countries where religion helps citizens not only to be legally correct but also morally upright. Indeed, citizens in such countries are encouraged to concentrate on the morality of their actions, in the sure belief that by doing so, they are unlikely to infringe any serious laws. We shall later consider the role that religion is playing in the Nigerian predicament.

In Nigeria, if the government does not go out of its way to produce good citizens, we may enquire with what success it has been producing happy citizens, even employing the narrow definition of happiness which assumes that material comfort is the sole basis of happiness. The provision of certain creature comforts is inevitable for the happiness of the citizens of a country. Citizens require a roof over their heads; they require a steady supply of energy, without which living in the twenty-first century is well-nigh unbearable; they require security; they need an abundant supply of water; and they need the assurance of an income which makes them live a decent life, however that is defined.

If these conditions for modern living are not provided by the government, the citizens, not surprisingly, embark on self-help. If the situation is serious enough, the provision of these necessities on a private basis becomes the passion that rules the citizens' life. Inevitably, the accumulation of sufficient wealth to enable the citizen to keep his head above water takes precedence over everything else. Materialism comes to rule the citizen's life, pushing into the periphery any concern for strict moral behaviour. Thus the roots of obsessive materialism in the modern day have to be traced very clearly to the inability of a government to ensure the minimum material comforts for the citizen. The resulting disequilibrium between materialism and morality is further aggravated by a rat race in which conspicuous consumption becomes glorified, further intensifying the spiral of obsessive materialism.

Materialism is a phenomenon that every society in the world has to cope with, and it is, naturally; exacerbated by the amount of wealth in the society and the methods of distribution of that wealth. Mediaeval Europe had little problem with materialism because the accumulation of wealth was not particularly a preoccupation. This is still the case in many parts of Africa and other parts of the developing world. But with industrialization in Europe and the discovery of mineral wealth in parts of Africa, materialism has come to assume a global dimension, so much so that the idea of a global village is being promoted by people who want to have for themselves as much of the wealth of the entire world as possible.

A personality test on the Internet provides the following among other main indices of materialism:

1. wealth seeking - i.e. the individual wants as much of the available wealth for himself or herself;
2. preferring extravagance i.e. the individual, wants to show off the amount of scealth they have succeeded in accumulating because they equate wealth with human worth;
3. selfish i.e. having no social conscience;
4. seeking status and power relative to peers — this refers to the competition and rivalry that goes on among people known in Nigeria as 'money bags';

5. regarding looking good as more important than comfort — i.e. preoccupation with appearance rather than reality;
6. manipulative — i.e. engaging in wheeling and dealing;
7. experiencing a need for applause — which, of course in reality, betrays an inferiority complex;
8. keen to win awards — evidence of a deep feeling of insecurity;
9. prefers instant gratification - which betrays a lack of profundity.

These indices are, of course, not to be regarded as absolutes, but each of them can be calibrated perhaps into a three way grading. Anyone possessing any of these traits to an appreciable degree can be regarded as being obsessively materialistic.

There are those, of course, who argue that obsessive materialism is the basis of capitalist democracy which has been imported into Nigeria, and find little wrong with it. Such people have, in admiration, commented on the dynamism of the Nigerian people, saying what wonderful go-getters they are. There have, to be sure, been experiments in socialism, in which materialism is reduced to the minimum and the government takes off the responsibility for providing the basic and modest material comforts of life from off the shoulders of the citizens. But these have become unfashionable since the collapse of the Soviet Union.,. However, the much-lauded free enterprise does encourage obsessive materialism even in countries which are admired by the developing countries, and the situation may get out of hand, as it appears to be doing in Nigeria the moment.

But why do many rulers in the developing countries Indulge in a shameless acquisition of wealth at the expense of their people, who are impoverished by their leaders' greed? It cannot be said that these leaders indulge in this behaviour in order to provide adequate material comforts for themselves. If anything, their countries ensure that they live in absolute luxury at no expense to themselves. So there have to be additional explanations for obsessive materialism among the elite, and particularly the rulers, in developing countries. One explanation is offered by JibriI in his classic lecture delivered to our Academy in 2003 (Jibril, 2005: 67), who cited Takaya (1997), who in turn cites All Mazrui as positing the theory of 'monarchical tendencies', which, according to Mazrui, explains why African leaders 'regard themselves as modern replacements of traditional rulers'. Indeed, most rulers in Africa see themselves as reincarnations of the heroic powerful ethnic lord of a bygone age who really was Lord 'of all that he surveyed, including the public treasury. Illusion of grandeur might be a more appropriate name for this affliction; but society, sadly, pays the price.

There is also the nouveau riche syndrome, which of course is by no means peculiar to developing countries.

The nouveaux riches would appear to be haunted by the memories of a poverty-stricken upbringing and the mortal fear of a relapse. They therefore feverishly accumulate wealth, enough not just to last their' own life time, but those of their children and grand-children as well. They, of course, usually suffer from poor or indifferent education.

Counting the cost of obsessive materialism can be rather depressing. Corruption, which in different degrees seems to be an inescapable feature of c:apita!ist democracy everywhere, becomes enlarged in developing countries such as Nigeria because there is little curb on the rapacity of the nouveaux riches, and no safety net for the genuinely indigent. It has been remarked,' with justification, that corruption has been structured into every facet of Nigerian life. &t it is not often emphasized that it is not a vice indulged in only by the high and mighty but also by the lowly citizens who apparently must be corrupt in order' to survive. The gateman at offices, the security man in public and private places, the policeman on the street - all fight to keep the wolf from the door by corruptly exploiting their fellow citizens. A Nigerian parliamentarian was once quoted to have said that the giving of gifts — a.k.a- bribes — was an important feature of traditional African culture which. should riot be interfered with. Indeed, Nigerians Would appear to be making a fetish of corruption resulting from obsessive materialism, for when economic necessity is added to cultural endorsement, it is indeed a Herculean task to try and stop it.

Obsessive materialism also promotes unwholesome social stratification. We are told that the middle class is in the process of being restored in, Nigeria. But the difference between the emerging middle class and the one which preceded it is very clear. The previous middle class consisted mainly of civil servants and teachers who were content with the moderate wages that they received. Now their ranks are being swamped by the new middle class in the private sector where full rein is given to materialism. The private sector is creaming off the best brains available in the country and there is a steady drift from public and educational establishments of people who want the best for themselves and their families. Perhaps it is even a misnomer to refer to this as the middle class since there is really no class above it. The stratification therefore is between this class and the rest of the country, most of whom earn only a fraction of the salaries in the private sector dominated by big business. This new class is being given every encouragement by the government in its desire to hand over the commanding heights of the economy to the private sector. This development is breeding social discontent and social antagonisms while stimulating higher degrees of obsessive materialism among the rest of society who, after all, do operate in the same economy. One prominent result of this is the unending demand for better salaries among the professional class who are struggling to hang on to the lower bands of the new middle class. They are what Jibril, (2005) would refer to as the sub-elite. The quiet rivalry between them and the elite proper is the source of much instability in the country because demands for better wages are all too often accompanied by industrial action.

But the place where many Nigerians would love to be is the National Assembly where, it would appear, our rulers live in a world of their own. Much investment is made in terms of bribery and even forgery, to be there. The pay is good, totally unrelated to what goes   on elsewhere in the   country, and the severance pay at   the   end   of   a   leisurely tenure of four years is unbelievable. The Vanguard of Monday, 28 May, 2007 carried this story:

> 'Governor Chimaroke Nnamani of Enugu State has released mouth-watering packages for members of the state House of Assembly whom he described as" conscientious sons and daughters" who boldly held their own stead in the course of the last segment of his administration.

> 'These packages (sic), which include the monetization of official residences and cars of the Honourable Members, as well as allocation of huge plots of land in the highbrow Independence Layout, Enugu, had the added monetary gestures of severance and

other   due   allowances,   among   other provisions.'

But perhaps this is even nothing compared with the l.uge expenditure, according to Jibril (op. cit.:85) in the first year of a parliamentarian's tenure. A careful computation by Jibril of expenditure from legitimate and other earnings brings the total figure to N83 million per parliamentarian for the first year alone. ,

No   one   who observes contemporary Nigerian manners,   and   pays   particular attention to the Nigerian newspapers, can fail to have noticed a sickening display of sycophancy which pervades social intercourse in Nigeria. Why is this so? Apologists might say that it is a carry-over 'from the culture of respect for age and position which is present in perhaps all the ethnic nationalities in the country. But there is an important difference. Deference for age and position is exhibited in the local cultures in a dignified and formulaic manner, except perhaps in dealing with natural ruler, in   which   case there is deliberate theatre. And in any case, no material reward is expected in return for such deference. Rather, it is all in an effort to keep the ruler in good mood and thus provide a form of social lubrication.

On the other hand, sycophancy in recent years has reached a shameless level, with individuals, patently harbouring clear and unmistakable motives, taking whole pages of newspapers to fawn over those from whom material reward is obviously expected because of their positions in society. This phenomenon has resulted in a general lack of respect for merit, for if you flatter those who supposedly matter sufficiently you can reach positions which you do not deserve while keeping out those who deserve them. The ultimate goal, of course, is the accumulation of wealth by any means imaginable. The resultant enthronement of mediocrity cannot be expected to aid the development of the country but rather gives further impetus to corruption.

There is great lamentation, honest or feigned, in the country about the falling standards of education in the country, and the gloomy picture was constantly painted by the last Minister of Education, who appeared genuinely outraged by the situation. But why should anyone put themselves through the strain of studying hard to emerge at the end with a good degree when there are less painful short-cuts to the accumulation of wealth, the assumed goal of human existence? As can be expected, this revulsion for sound education is more prevalent among those male students who are sure they can make their way to the top through a combination of cheating, corruption and sycophancy. So unerringly is the future of the country being mortgaged.

What is happening to education should be a cause for great concern to everyone in the country. Reports from secondary schools speak of finely developed methods of cheating in the school certificate examinations, with cell phones now being pressed into service to relay answers surreptitiously to candidates in examination halls. Why cell phones should be allowed in examination halls in the first place beats one's imagination. It simply shows the scant regard in which transparency is held generally in the country. Jibril (op. ct.) reports that:

'In 2004.. .the Joint Admissions and Matriculation Board (JAMB) had to cancel the results of some 116,000 candidates who were involved in examination malpractice.'

The figures have probably gone up in the last two years.

Then many of those who fail the examinations in spite of strenuous attempts to cheat at that level turn up at the universities with fake results sold to them by some officials of the Joint Admissions and Matriculation Board. These results are bought, we are told, on behalf of the students by their parents, no less! And an even more bewildering revelation is that such parents sometimes find collaborators in some universities which, themselves, should be looking for the very best candidates for admission.

The reason for this is the craze for certificates in the country as an aid to securing undeserved jobs. It is believed that, as a result, there are very many forged certificates in circulation in the country, even, as we have found, among the country's rulers. The scam has now been sent a notch higher by people who overnight adopt the title of

'Doctor' — presumably of philosophy or even 'Professor'; and hotels in the country lend their premises, obviously for a fee, to the staging of fake graduation ceremonies where doctorate degrees — including higher doctorates - are freely sold. There appear to be no limits to the extent to which some people will go to get where they do not deserve to be, in an effort not to be left behind in the rat race. In the process, scholarship is made a mockery of.

Anyone who owns an email address must find that they are besieged on a daily basis by people at pains to swindle them, and the persistence of this scam suggests that there are people gullible enough, or more correctly, desperate enough — to be taken in by it. Names of Ministers and high government officials are falsely but freely used to deceive the unwary gambler, without any consideration for what this does to the image of the country which, in any case, is already regarded as one of the most corrupt in the world. The standard gambit, unimaginatively repeated in mail after mail, is the story of a person, quite often a female, who has access to millions of dollars which only they know about, and which they are prepared to share with their correspondent if the latter would be so kind as to furnish the writer with the details of their bank accounts. I wonder how many Nigerians have fallen for this cheap trick.

Another wage of obsessive materialism, of the disequilibrium between morality and materialism in human conduct in Nigeria, is the traffic in human beings. Again, this is not a Nigerian original idea, but the ruthlessness with which it is pursued boggles the mind. The Vanguard of Wednesday, 30 May, 2007 carried the following story. I crave your indulgence to quote it in full and unedited to preserve its flavour:

'A human-trafficking syndicate with the kingpins in Libya has been uncovered at Uro-Irri community area of Delta State.

'Trouble started for the Syndicate when the family of the girl in question, Miss Oregbor, a secondary
school dropout, aged between ?5-27 years from Idheze community, who was trafficked to Libya, confronted the contact men who were resident in the town.

'She was said to have been taken to Libya by the syndicate without the knowledge of her fiancé
who had been taking care of her and her sick father.

'Few months after the girl left the shores or Nigeria, the two contact men received some monetary compensation from the kingpins of-the
syndicate with which they purchased motorcycles and started moulding blocks for their respective
buildings.

'A concerned native, Gowon Adebe, who smelt a rat all along, got information that she was trafficked by the syndicate and in conjunction with the family members of the girl, they confronted the middle men, who demanded for (sic) N1 million, being their expenses in trafficking the girl abroad before they would work for her return back to the country.

'He reportedly petitioned the police in Delta State and the two suspects were picked up. They allegedly confessed their role in the human trafficking syndicate and entered an undertaking that they would produce her in two weeks time but they failed to deliver

'According to Adebe: "When I contacted them, the two entered an undertaking with me that they were going to ensure the return of the girl and that I should give them one week, so after one week, I called them and they told me that

because they spent so much money on the girl, I should provide million if I am so much interested on the girl's return

' "They asked Why am interested in the matter, that after all, the girl in question is not my relation but if I so desire her return, I should provide the money.

' "I told them human trafficking is an offence and an abomination in Isoko, and I will not close my eyes because I have children and I don't want such a thing to happen to any member of my family or my town"

All this is redolent of the trans-Atlantic slave trade of the seventeenth and eighteenth centuries, but even the slavers of that era did not make monetary demands on the slaves' relations! But also, there is a picture of abject poverty evoked by the story. As soon as the slavers collected the money, they proceeded immediately to buy motor cycles and begin the foundations of the buildings of their personal homes. It portrays' what human beings would do to solve their existential problems in a society 'that they believe does not care for them. How, by the way, did the slavers expect rustic villagers in a remote region of Nigeria to come up with N1 million?

There have, to be sure, been spirited attempts to defend what has here been referred to as obsessive materialism, and one of the best known is that by Andrew Carnegie in his thought-provoking article, entitled, appropriately, Wealth (Carnegie, 1889). Carnegie in the very first sentence of the article (p. 1) provides his solution to the problem posed by wealth.

'The problem of our age,' he declares solemnly, 'is the proper administration of wealth, so that the ties of brotherhood may still bind together the rich and the poor in harmonious relationship.'

Notice that Carnegie is not concerned with the eradication of poverty, but with ways of making the rich and the poor live together harmoniously. Carnegie believes that the disparity in society is brought about by the 'law of competition,' which, he believes, is 'not only beneficial, but essential for the future progress of the race.'

Carnegie reserves some scathing remarks for those he termed 'socialists and anarchists', the two terms presumably referring to the same group of people as far as Carnegie is concerned. He says (p. 7):

> 'The Socialist or Anarchist who seeks to overturn' the present conditions is to be regarded as attacking the foundation upon which civilization itself rests, for civilization took its start from the day that the capable, industrious workman said to his incompetent and lazy fellow, "if thou dost now sow, thou shalt not reap," and thus ended the primitive Communism by separating the drones from the bees. One who studies this subject will soon be brought face to face with the conclusion that upon the sacredness of property

civilization itself depends — the right of the labourer to his hundred dollars in the savings bank, and equally the legal right of the millionaire to his millions. To those who propose to substitute Communism for this intense Individualism the answer therefore is:
The race has tried that. All progress from that barbarous day to the present has resulted from its displacement. Not evil, but good, has come to the race from the accumulation of wealth by those who have the ability and energy that produce it.'

There could not have been a better manifesto for capitalism, and for the obsessive materialism that goes along with it. Carnegie adds, for good measure:

'...the law of accumulation of wealth, and the law of Competition are the highest results of human experience, the soil in which society so far has produced the best fruit. Unequally or unjustly, perhaps, as these laws sometimes operate, and imperfect as they appear to the Idealist, they are, nevertheless, like the highest type of man, the best and most

valuable of. all that humanity has
yet accomplished.'

Carnegie was writing, of course, before the rise of communism in Eastern Europe, but it is doubtful if his views would have been altered by the rise and sp9ctacular fall of that system.

We may wonder just how much all this is applicable to the present situation in Nigeria. Is the accumulation of enormous wealth in the hands of those who possess it in the country today, a result of fair competition? The wealthy people of America in Carnegie's day were really gifted industrialists and talented businessmen who literally created their wealth. I do not think that lucky winners of sweepstakes would have properly qualified, though undoubtedly there must have been a few, who in any case squandered the windfall as fast as it came their way. Public officers do not come under this category either, and this is still true today: American congressmen do not' belong in the. same leagye as Bill Gates. But in Nigeria, Assemblymen and politicianstend to. be among

the wealthiest in the country, riot just because of the comparatively large remunerations that they receive but, more importantly, because of the access that they have to contracts and sundry windfalls. This is little different from winning sweepstakes, and this accounts for the alarming reckles spending that goes on in the country. This results in inflation, and the rest of 'society has, perforce, to be in turn obsessively materialistic to cope. Whatever competition there is, is largely unfair competition The Nigerian bee Is of a different species from the American one referred to by Carnegie.

We may wonder Why this is so; and the answer is provided in Carnegie's article. There is a firm religious underpinning to the American society. It is worth quoting him once again(p 18):

> 'The highest life is probably to be reached, not by such imitation of the life of Christ as Count Tolstoy gives us, but, while animated by Christ's spirit, by recognizing the changed conditions of this age, and adopting modes of expressing this spirit suitable to the changed conditions under which we live; still labouring for the good of our fellows, which was the essence of His life and teaching, but labouring in a different manner.'

In essence, for Carnegie, nothing has really changed since mediaeval times: the relation between the rich and the poor, for him, is analogous to the relationship between the lord and his serf. The only difference is that the poor of today (or, more accurately, of Carnegie's day) are better off materially than the mediaeval serf. The lord took care of his serf as he was enjoined to do by his religion; and similarly the modern wealthy man must look after the poor, especially those working for him. It is easy to see how strongly this philosophy holds in the United States of America, producing, apart from Carnegie himself, such other notable wealthy individuals as Rockefeller, Ford, Bill Gates and McArthur, among many others; and it is possible to argue that this philosophy has been substantially responsible for the phenomenal success of their country. We may n1ote that, from, giving succor to the poor in their own country, they have even gone out to reach the poor of the world.

I referred earlier to the role of religion, which would have been expected to exert similar moderating and compassionate influence on wealthy individuals in Nigeria. Morality, after all, is expected to be the particular forte of religions. Observers in recent years have commented on the state of religion in the country, and their comments have seldom been flattering. If we may take Christianity as an example, there has, to be sure, been phenomenal growth in the physical building" of Churches across the country, and a visitor to the country may be forgiven for assuming that Nigeria is a very religious country. Church signboards can be seen in most cities within a few meters of one another and, judging by these signboards, there may well be more Christian sects and denominations in the country than anywhere else in the whole world. But all this, to what effect? It has misled a recent international poll into awarding the palm to Nigeria in the sphere of religion. The country is indeed replete with Bishops, some of them self-appointed, and there are pastors and evangelists galore. In terms of membership, the evidence is equally impressive. There are, in particular, legions of self-proclaimed 'born again' Christians. Indeed, it has been remarked that religion is one of the fastest-growing businesses in the country.

All this raises the question of an appropriate definition of religion. Should it really be a 'business'? Or has obsessive materialism found its way even to the sacred precincts of places of worship?

Of course, there has always been a business side to religion. Since mediaeval times, the Church in Europe has owned landed property and even financial institutions. But the question is what it has traditionally done with the wealth thus accumulated. As we know, it has been used principally for the expansion of Christianity throughout the world; and Nigeria itself has been a beneficiary of this policy. The personnel themselves have had have access to the wealth and, in the Roman Catholic Church, for example, the priests even receive no salaries and live a very simple life.

At the same time, the Church has, traditionally, maintained the focus on making men and women better human beings by urging them to live by the doctrines of the Faith, which has been summarized as follows:

> 'The first commandment is this: ..You shall love the Lord your God with all your heart, with all your soul, with all your mind, and with all you strength. The second is this: Love your neighbour as yourself. There is no other commandment greater than these.'

The other major religion in Nigeria, Islam, subscribes to the same ideal. There, praying seven times a day and the giving of alms are two major pillars of the religion.

With respect to Christianity, a great change has come about in recent years following, particularly, developments in the United States of America. The business side of religion has come to the fore, and genuine attempts to save souls by making men and women better human beings are in danger of being subverted by the raising of funds and other materialistic pursuits. Individuals now establish Churches, just as one would establish a business, and a new strain of Christianity referred to as prosperity Christianity is taking hold on the imagination, not only of its preachers, but, more ominously, of the congregation. The Scripture is being re-interpreted to say that God in fact intends everyone to be wealthy, and the impression is created in some cases that if you are not wealthy, it must be that you are not a good Christian of course, the preachers themselves are the very picture of prosperity. The flock is being led to forget the parable of the Rich Fool, and thus obsessive materialism receives the blessing of the Church. Theatricality by preachers, all too often, is substituted for piety, and the impression grows that, unlike in the past, religion is now made to sustain business, instead of business being made to sustain religion. Denominations measure their success, not in terms of the quality of Christians they produce, but of the number of physical structures thy have managed to put up, even with money from questionable sources.

The Church receives the generous offerings of its wealthy members, whom it treats deferentially, even when it is known that the source of such wealth is suspect. Those who are yet to be wealthy are promised miracles to fulfil their hearts' desires.

Meanwhile, what happens to what should be the congregation's preoccupation with human goodness? It is replaced by what admittedly is an impressive knowledge of the Bible. But it is doubtful if souls are saved simply by the ability to quote the Bible with great facility and declare oneself 'born again'. What this breeds is hypocrisy, not true religion. The in-thing is to serve both God and Mammon, with the latter having the upper hand.

Fortunately, not all the Churches in the country present this disturbing image. There are still Churches which are faithful to their stewardship, which are concerned with relating the teachings of the Church to the problems of the daily living of the members of their congregations. But the voices of the preachers in such Churches are increasingly drowned by the strident proclamations of the prosperity preachers. The danger is that more and more Churches may become dazzled by the material success of the prosperity preachers, and tempted to conform, if only to prevent being deserted by their own congregations. This is a matter that the respected Christian Association of Nigeria should, ponder most prayerfully.

Another agency which should play a vital role in the moderation of obsessive materialism is the education system. A good education system cannot be expected to produce a bad society; but unfortunately, it is equally true that a bad society cannot produce a good education system either. The culture that obtains in schools cannot be expected to be radically different from that which prevails in the larger society. But a progressive society does take care that the coming generations are better than the existing ones.

The primary and secondary levels are particularly important. If society fails to impart the right moral values in children at this stage, it is not likely that the children will pick them up elsewhere. Religion may, to some extent, come to the rescue. This indeed is why, historically, schools were founded and administered by religious bodies, and the story is no different in this country. But later in Europe, in the nineteenth century, governments came to regard the education of children as one of their major responsibilities, and the majority of schools came to be run by the State. But since, in Europe, the State itself — and particularly the ruling classes - was already imbued with Christian values, the education of children continued to be conducted in the most responsible manner, and there was adequate supervision.

Similarly in Nigeria, the first schools were founded by the two religious bodies in the country — Christian and Islamic. And when the colonial government decided, partly in response to the fashion in Europe, and partly for its own selfish reasons, to take responsibility for education, it did so rather cautiously, allowing the religious bodies to carry on as proprietors but supporting them with grants in aid. That way, the moral content of education was not jeopardized. Access was admittedly very limited, but those who managed to go to school received good education.

Trouble started when the various governments, in the Second Republic, decided to expand access, which in itself was a laudable idea. But the deterioration that followed the consequent take-over of all schools by the governments, in both the intellectual and moral tone of schools, is now well documented and well known. Yet it is taking a lot of persuading to get some governments to return to the previous mode of running schools. If the new private/public policy of school proprietorship will result in such a return, it would be a welcome development, at least until such a time as society proves itself worthy of exclusively running the institutions.

It is, however, unfortunate that even the religious organizations that did such a good job in the past seem to have lost the zeal to operate schools. Some of them have reluctantly taken back secondary schools when given the opportunity to do so, usually as the result of the persistent efforts of the old boys and girls of such schools, but it does not seem that primary schools are being taken back in any large numbers, if at all. Yet this is the crucial tier for rebuilding the moral tone of the entire society. The initiative in this area would appear now to be left, for good or ill, to private individual proprietors. The religious bodies' priorities would appear to lie elsewhere. And yet, it would be very sad indeed if education has lost its former high priority in the preoccupations of religious bodies, perhaps yielding pride of place to more materialistic endeavours'.

Another important possible moderating influence on obsessive materialism is the effect of role models whether in historical or contemporary perspectives. India had Mahatma Gandhi; Singapore had Lee Kwan Yew; Tanzania had Julius Nyerere; South Africa has Nelson Mandela; and some other countries similarly had leaders who by their personal example captured the imagination of their countrymen, and indeed of the whole world, and transformed the moral fibre of their countries. Unfortunately in Nigeria, there is hardly any commanding figure that can be held up as a shining example of sobriety, as one who is prepared to render sacrificial service to the fatherland. This is not surprising, as Nigeria pampers its leaders with material comforts, smothering them with adulation in the hope of material reward. Perhaps this is what people mean when they say that Nigeria is still waiting for the Messiah.

Yet, as Jibril (op. cit.) remarks with justification, the three founding fathers of the country, with all their faults, approximated more closely to the ideal than contemporary leaders. The dreadful combination of mineral oil and military governance of the country would appear to have installed an era of giddy materialism in the country in which the leaders lead the way. Never has it been more clearly and energetically demonstrated that the labourer is worthy of his hire — indeed, more than worthy. There is no originality in the remark that the problems that plague Nigeria are largely leadership problems.

Surely, no country in the modern world can survive without the requisite dose of materialism; but at the same time, it is doubtful if a country can survive if it lives for nothing but materialism. In a world dominated by Gross Domestic Product and similar indices of development, a government has to pay due attention to the creature comforts of its citizens; but this need not be made an end in itself. The end should rather be the cultivation of more refined citizens in search of higher ideals. If we may return, in closing, to Carnegie, he lived in a country where the government ensured free and fair competition; where, by and large, every citizen was encouraged to develop his or her potential to the limit. It was in this kind of environment that Carnegie was able to make his immense wealth in the steel industry and experienced self-fulfillment. His particular forte was the creation of wealth, and society allowed him to develop his potential legitimately and to the fullest. But the accumulation of wealth did not make Carnegie less of a moral human being. He believed strongly that his wealth was held in trust for society at large, and that his surplus should be ploughed back to society in areas where it was likely to be most productive. He felt that in this way, the general level of well-being in society would be raised, and he particularly emphasized the pleasures of the

intellect rather than of the body. It is perhaps
appropriate to give him the last word in this lecture
(Carnegie, 1889:24):

> '..the man who dies
> leaving behind him
> millions of available
> wealth, which was
> his to administer
> during life, will pass
> away "unwept,
> unhonoured, and
> unsung," no matter
> to what uses he
> leaves the dross
> which he cannot
> take with him. Of
> such as these the
> public verdict will
> then be: "The man
> who dies thus rich
> dies disgraced."

REFERENCES

Bentham, Jeremy (1789)
introduction to the Principles of
Morals and Legislation.

Carnegie A. (1889) Wealth. North
American Review. CXLVII

Jibril, Munzali (2005) 'Is there Not,
amongst You, A Righteous

Man?': The
Nigerian Factor And The Nigerian
Condition. In Ogude S.
(ed)   Public Morality and the
Nigerian Polity. Ibadan:
Occasional Publication of the
Nigerian Academy of Letters: 56-
92.
Jones, R. Moral Philosophy.
www.philosopher.org.uk/moral.htm

Kant, I. (1953) A Critique of Pure
Reason. London: Macmillan.

www.ingramcontent.com/pod-product-compliance
Lightning Source LLC
Chambersburg PA
CBHW050526290526
45786CB00007B/2710